PERRIER GUIDE TO THE
ITALIAN MENU

READER'S DIGEST

perrier

GUIDE TO THE

ITALIAN

MENU

Contributor and adviser
Simone Lavarini

Contributing editor
Lizzie Boyd

PUBLISHED BY
THE READER'S DIGEST
ASSOCIATION LIMITED
LONDON NEW YORK MONTREAL
SYDNEY CAPE TOWN

Perrier/Reader's Digest Guide to the Italian Menu was edited and designed by The Reader's Digest Association Limited, London

Printed in Great Britain

CONTENTS

FOREWORD

Italian restaurants through the world unfailingly offer the popular specialities of spaghetti and other pasta dishes, of pizzas, veal escalopes and zabaglione, but there is a great deal more to discover from Italy's vast cuisine. The grand banquets of Imperial Rome are a thing of the past, and little more than historical records has survived from the Lucullan feasts where ostentatious presentation far outranked the gastronomic contents. Any visitor to Italy is unlikely to come across wild boar stuffed with live thrushes, like the one Trimalchio, during the reign of Nero, is reputed to have served to his guests. But in northern Italy and on Sardinia, thrushes grilled with aromatic herbs remain a popular delicacy; in Piedmont they offer *cinghiale in agrodolce*, roast boar with a rich sauce which is sharpened with vinegar and sweetened with chocolate and which bears a close resemblance to the honey and vinegar sauces with which the ancient Romans disguised their food.

Caesar's armies trampled their way across Europe on little more than their daily ration of *pulmentum* or *polenta* – millet served up as a liquid porridge or baked to hard loaves. Today, *polenta* is still the staple diet in northern Italy, though maize has replaced the millet.

With the fall of the Roman empire, sumptuous living sank into oblivion, to reappear centuries later when Venice emerged as the chief trading port. Venice's fortunes were founded on her salt works, from which developed a brisk trade in salted fish. Today any self-respecting Venetian restaurant will feature one of the city's specialities: *baccala alla Vicentina*, salt cod cooked with milk and onions. During the Renaissance the culinary arts flourished

Simone Lavarini began his training in Italy in 1943. Arriving in London in 1949, via Switzerland and France, he established several successful Italian restaurants and is co-director of La Bussola.

anew; in Florence the doges outdid each other with great banquets which approached those of ancient Rome in splendour, none more so than those at the palaces of the Medicis. When, in 1533, Catherine di Medici left her native Florence for France, to become the wife of the future Henry II, she naturally brought with her a train of skilled cooks. They introduced to France delicate sweet pastries, stuffed succulent poultry and meat, dainty vegetable dishes and refreshing ices. The French readily absorbed the arts of the Italian chefs, improved and perfected them to what is now known as the *haute cuisine.*

Meanwhile in Italy, the Italians continued to develop their own, highly individual cuisine, with strong differences from region to region reflecting local produce and local prosperity – or lack of it. In the north, the fertile lands of Veneto yield plump asparagus, tangy wild mushrooms and *radicchio rosso* (red chicory); scampi and spider crabs come from the Adriatic sea, and San Daniele ham is said to rival *prosciutto* from Parma. Lombardy has the richest dairy and agriculture industries; the rice fields in the Po Valley are evident in such dishes as *risotto* and *minestrone alla Milanese*. Gorgonzola, which originates in Lombardy, goes into another Milanese speciality: pears stuffed with Gorgonzola cheese and walnuts.

Bologna, home of salamis and mortadella sausages and of the large black and white truffles which adorn many a tagliatelle dish, is the centre of the cheese industry, and huge Parmesan cheeses are made to centuries-old recipes. Tuscany excels with beef and pork dishes, cooked in local olive oil and flavoured with wild rosemary from the pastures. The famous *brodetto*, a thick fish stew, resembles the Genoese *burrida*, and Florence claims as her own *risotto nero* of cuttlefish and rice coloured black with the ink.

In Rome all culinary roads come together, with plenty of local specialities, such as *abbachio*, milk-fed baby lamb spit-roasted with rosemary. There are delectable little potato dumplings, known as *gnocchi*, dribbling with butter and melted cheese, and the fascinating *suppli al telefono* – golden, crisp-fried rice balls stuffed with mozzarella cheese which pulls out like thin telephone wires as the cheese melts. *Saltimbocca*, of veal and ham olives cooked in wine, is typically Roman and so are tender young artichokes deep-fried in olive oil (*carciofi alla Giudea*).

Naples, in southern Italy, poor in comparison with the fertile north, has left her indilutable mark on Italian – and international – cuisine with her pizzas and her pastas, her ice-creams and water ices.

The Italians grasp any opportunity, and especially the many religious festivals, to celebrate with food and wine. Carnival in February is synonymous with *Torrone* and *Cannoli Siciliana*, both sweet concoctions, the former rich with nougat, the latter with ricotta cheese, candied peel and nuts. Easter is celebrated with spit-roasted kid and a light fairy cake known as *Colomba*, while typical Christmas dishes include *Panettone*, an aromatic brioche filled with raisins and candied fruit.

Most Italians breakfast lightly, lunch at any time between noon and early afternoon and dine leisurely from early to late evening. There are eating establishments of all types: the *Tavola Caldas* are popular for their quick stand-up or sit-down midday meals, with a choice of hot or cold bread rolls, *Tremezzini* (sandwiches), rice balls and meat dishes from the counter. At the *Trattorias* (restaurants) lunch and dinner are enjoyed at leisure, a menu typically consisting of a first course, a main dish and a sweet. Wine is the usual drink, with local carafe wines being reasonably priced and of good quality; a bottle of mineral water is ever present at each table. Many *Pizzerias* stay open until late into the night, and after theatre and cabaret time they are thronged with customers munching their favourite pizzas. In the mornings, Italians frequent bars and cafés for *espresso* or *cappuccino* coffee, with a small brioche or cake, but at any time of day they need no excuse for stepping inside for a snack and a drink. Every village and town has its favourite bars, which are the social gathering places for gossip and arguments.

It was between the two World Wars that Italian restaurants began to appear in earnest in England, introducing such delicacies as scampi, Parma ham (*prosciutto*), cannelloni, *Cassata Siciliana*, soft ice-cream and water ices. Although these restaurants were in the upper price bracket, the popularity of Italian food grew to such an extent that by the mid-1950s Italian-style espresso coffee bars had become an accepted feature of London life. They were soon followed by the pizza establishments and spaghetti houses, which are now found in every high street.

ANTIPASTI

Antipasti, the Italian term for appetisers, are served prior to the soup course. Sometimes they consist merely of a selection of crisp vegetables or thin slices of salamis, to be nibbled at with drinks. Sometimes they are more substantial, like *Prosciutto di Parma e melone* (or *fichi*) – Parma ham with melon (or fresh figs), and *Insalata di riso e gamberetti* (rice and shrimp salad), or *Lumache al maggiordomo* (snails in garlic sauce). Tunny fish is popular and appears in combination with fresh or cooked vegetables and dressed with oil and lemon juice; or mixed with mayonnaise and spooned over eggs (*Uova tonnato*).

1

1 **Fritto misto di mare**
MIXED SEAFOOD
of deep-fried whitebait,
baby soles, red mullet,
scampi, prawns and strips
of squid, garnished with
lemon quarters. Originally
from the Genoan water
front and now a popular
item on most restaurant
menus

2 **Antipasto misto**
MIXED HORS D'OEUVRE
or tit-bits of crisp celery
sticks and radishes, tunny
fish and sardines, thinly
sliced salami and pimentos,
garnished with black and
green, stuffed olives. Slices
of mortadella sausage and
smoked ham are often
included

2

SOUPS

Top row, from left Riso e prezzemolo in brodo: BEEF BROTH WITH RICE; Zuppa alla Pavese: CONSOMMÉ WITH EGG AND PARMESAN *Bottom* Crema di crostacei vecchia Romana: CREAM OF SHELLFISH SOUP; Pasta e

Italian soups are hearty affairs, especially the minestrones – thick vegetable soups with pasta or rice, given various regional touches as in the *pesto*-flavoured *Minestrone alla Genovese*. Plain broth or consommés (*brodo*) are usually substantiated with pasta, lentils or rice, or with small dumplings of minced chicken (*Budino di pollo in brodo*). Try the popular *Stracciatella* of hot chicken broth mixed with eggs, semolina and Parmesan cheese. Chunky fish soups, known as *brodetto* or *burrida* (see pages 20–21) are more stews than soups.

fagioli: WHITE BEANS AND PASTA SOUP; Minestrone alla Milanese: VEGETABLE, PORK AND PASTA SOUP

PASTA DISHES

There are more than 50 types of pasta, the
traditional Italian dish. Though they differ in shapes
and sizes, the chief distinction is between fresh,
home-made pasta (*pasta fatta in casa*) and the mass-
produced kinds. The majority is made from durum
wheat and water, but eggs go into tagliatelli, lasagne
and ravioli, the collective term for stuffed pasta.
Spinach may also be added, for flavour and colour,
and pasta then becomes *verde*. Some names are
simply regional variants; tagliatelli, for instance, is
fettuccine in Rome, while in Tuscany it is pappardelle
(it is used as the border in the picture below).

1 PASTA TYPES INCLUDE *conchiglie* (shells), *farfalle* (bows), spaghetti (in the centre), *fuselli* (spirals), *penne* (short maccheroni) and *tagliatelli* (white or green ribbon noodles with eggs). Tiny *stelle* (stars) and *conchigliette* are used as garnishes; *lasagne*, bottom left, is baked

2 Spaghetti napoli
SPAGHETTI WITH TOMATO, ONION AND GARLIC SAUCE

3 Spaghetti con le melanzane
SPAGHETTI WITH SAUTÉ AUBERGINES

4 Pappardelle con la lepre
RIBBON NOODLES WITH HARE SAUCE; Tuscan speciality

5

6

5 Cannelloni al forno
STUFFED PASTA TUBES BAKED
IN TOMATO AND CREAM
SAUCE

6 Tortellini di spinaci e
ricotta, burro e salvia
PASTA RINGS STUFFED WITH
SPINACH AND RICOTTA
CHEESE,
with butter and sage

7 Lasagne verde al forno
BAKED GREEN LASAGNE
WITH RAGOÛT AND
BÉCHAMEL SAUCE

8 Ravioli Genovese
STUFFED PASTA SQUARES

9 Taglierini al pesto
FINE RIBBON NOODLES WITH
BASIL AND GARLIC SAUCE

RISOTTOS AND PIZZAS

In northern Italy, rice is as important as pasta is in the south. Cooked in butter or oil, with stock or wine, it is served *bianco*, plain, or mixed with vegetables, seafood, meat or cheese. Pizzas are known throughout the world. The base is a yeast dough, though *Pizza rustica*, from southern Italy, is made with shortcrust and resembles a quiche. The *pizzeria*, inexpensive taverns, specialise in hot pizzas, with any number of fillings, including *con cozze*, with mussels, and *con vongole*, with clams. The Neapolitan *Calzone* is a kind of half-moon pizza filled with ham and mozzarella cheese.

1 Risotto di pesci
FISH RISOTTO,
cooked in wine with
shrimps and green peas,
garnished with pimentos
and anchovy fillets

2 Pizza Napoletana
NEAPOLITAN PIZZA.
The classic pizza, with
mozzarella cheese,
anchovies, tomatoes,
oregano and olives

3 Pizza margherita
SIMILAR TO NAPOLETANA,
but flavoured with basil
instead of oregano, and
with Parmesan cheese

4 Pizza con tutto
HOUSE SPECIALITY

2

3

4

FISH

Next to pasta, fish ranks as Italy's most important food. From the sea comes mullet, sole, sea bass and tunny fish among many others, and huge catches of anchovies and sardines, together with oysters, clams mussels and spiny lobsters. Venice claims the scampi as its own, serving it *alla griglia*, grilled with garlic butter; another Venetian speciality is *Anguilles marinata*, eel marinated in red wine and oil, and *Baccala mantecata*, creamed salt cod. Everywhere are local fish stews, like the famed *Brodetto* of Ravenna, similar to Genoese *burrida*, but with fish and soup served separately.

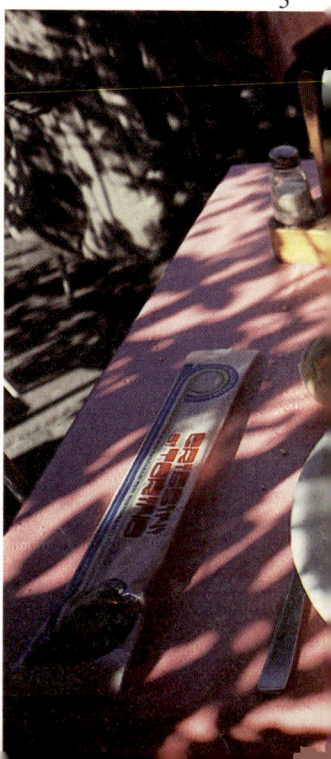

1 Calamari in umido
   SQUID STEW IN RED WINE,
   with tomatoes, onions,
   garlic and herbs

2 Sogliola burro capperi
   GRILLED SOLE WITH BROWN
   BUTTER
   flavoured with vinegar and
   capers

3 Burrida
   GENOESE FISH STEW
   of white fish, eel, squid and
   shellfish, with tomatoes,
   garlic and herbs

4 Triglia alla Livornese
   GRILLED RED MULLET WITH
   TOMATO AND GARLIC SAUCE

SHELLFISH

1

Shellfish include the strange little mussels known from their shape as sea dates (*datteri di mare*). They are found along the Genoese coasts and go into *Zuppa di cozze*, a thick mussels broth with herbs, oil, white wine and tomatoes, served with grated lemon peel. Lobster (*aragosta*) is plainly grilled, but accompanied by *pesto*, that sharp basil and garlic sauce. Squid, cuttlefish and octopus are popular in stews, seafood cocktails and mixed fries; *Calamaretti fritti*, deep-fried baby squid, appear on many an hors d'oeuvre menu.

1 Cacciucco alla Genovese
FISH STEW OF SQUID,
MUSSELS, CLAMS AND
SHRIMPS
in tomato, parsley and garlic sauce

2 Scampi fritti
DEEP-FRIED SCAMPI WITH
REMOULADE SAUCE AND
LEMON GARNISH

POULTRY AND GAME

The Arno Valley in Tuscany is said to breed the best chicken and to serve them most succulently, after grilling over a charcoal fire. Elsewhere, *petti di pollo* (chicken breasts) are popular dishes whether *alla valdostana*, with white truffles and a wine sauce, or *alla Bolognese*, sauté chicken topped with Parma ham and grated Parmesan. Duck (*anitra*), wild boar (*cinghiale*) and hare (*lepre*) feature *in agrodolce*, a sweet and sour sauce. Small game and song birds (*uccellette*) are common, either grilled or roasted and often served with crisp fritters of *polenta* (maize flour porridge) flavoured with cheese.

1 Pollo alla diavola
GRILLED SPRING CHICKEN
Cooked over charcoals in
Tuscany, basted with oil
and ground ginger

2 Pollo alla cacciatora
CHICKEN BRAISED IN WINE,
TOMATOES AND MUSHROOMS.
Sometimes with anchovy
and black olive sauce

3 Quaglie con risotto
QUAIL BRAISED IN WINE,
served on a bed of buttered
rice garnished with
mushrooms

4 Tordi arrosto con pancetta
e rosmarino
ROAST SKEWERED THRUSHES
AND PARMA SALAMI
FLAVOURED WITH ROSEMARY

MEAT

The meat dishes of Italy are generally of fine quality,
notably veal from Lombardy, beef from Tuscany
and pork from Emilia – *Arista Fiorentina* is a
succulent, slow-roasted loin of pork with garlic,
cloves and rosemary. It is usually served cold, like
many other classic dishes, such as *Maiale al latte*,
pork cooked in milk, and *Vitello tonnato*, leg of veal
stuffed with anchovies and served with tunny fish
mayonnaise. Herbs and wine are used for braising
stuffed veal or beef olives, escalopes and cutlets.
Parma ham (*prosciutto*) is well known, along with
salami and mortadella pork sausages from Bologna.

1

3

2

4

5

6

7

10

8

9

7 Polenta e luganega
SPICY SAUTÉ PORK SAUSAGES
SERVED WITH POLENTA

8 Polpettine alla Fiorentina
MEAT RISSOLES

9 Zampone con lenticchie
STUFFED PIGS' TROTTERS
WITH BROWN LENTILS

10 Bollito misto con mostarda
di Cremona
MIXED BOILED MEATS WITH
BRAISED VEGETABLES AND
MUSTARD FRUIT CHUTNEY

11 Costoletta di vitello alla
valdostana
SAUTÉ VEAL CUTLET STUFFED
WITH FONTINA CHEESE

11

VEGETABLES

Many vegetables are served as first courses, hot or cold, before the meat. Lightly boiled to the *al dente* stage, beans, carrots, spinach, broccoli and leeks are dressed with oil and lemon juice, ham, bacon, anchovies, pine kernels and herbs. There is a Roman speciality of *Carciofi alla giudea* – crisp, deep-fried globe artichokes – and a Venetian one, *Carciofi alla Veneziana*, of small violet artichokes braised in oil and white wine. *Tartufi bianchi* (white truffles) are unique to Italian cuisine: grated they top risottos, pastas and salads, sliced they lend distinctive flavour to veal, chicken and cheese dishes.

1

1 Punti di asparagi alla
  Milanese
  BUTTERED ASPARAGUS TIPS
  TOPPED WITH FRIED EGGS

2 Caponata alla Siciliana
  SAUTÉ AUBERGINES IN
  SWEET-SOUR TOMATO SAUCE
  WITH CELERY, ANCHOVIES,
  CAPERS AND OLIVES.
  Served cold

3 Peperoni ripieni
  BAKED GREEN PEPPERS
  STUFFED WITH RICE,
  MUSHROOMS AND TOMATOES,
  shrimp risotto and chopped
  ham and chicken in cheese
  sauce

SALADS

The usual accompaniment to main course dishes is a side salad (*insalata*), either mixed (*mista*) or green (*verde*), potato salad (*Insalata di patate*) tossed in oil, lemon juice, garlic and raw onion rings, or a tomato salad dressed only with oil, seasoning and fresh basil (*Insalata di pomodori e basilico*). Most other salads are served as first courses, such as *Peperonata*, a substantial dish of sweet peppers and tomatoes cooked with onion and garlic in oil and served cold. A recent introduction to Britain is *Radicchio di Treviso*, an attractive, crimson and crisp type of cos lettuce, with a light bitter taste.

1 Insalata di pomodori
TOMATO SALAD GARNISHED
WITH FRESH MUSHROOMS,
SALAD ONIONS, WATERCRESS
AND BLACK OLIVES

2 Insalate e antipasti
SIDE SALADS AND HORS
D'OEUVRE
typically include mozzarella
cheese and tomatoes (front row), next to grilled
aubergines and sauté
mushrooms. Behind a
pepper and anchovy salad,
courgettes in garlic
dressing, artichokes in
lemon juice, and tunny fish
salad. In the third row are
marinated sardines with
lake trout, and mushroom
salad

CHEESES

Italian cuisine is unthinkable without *Parmigiano reggiano* (*grana*), known the world over as Parmesan. Other cooking cheeses are Mozzarella, popular for pizzas; Ricotta, a moist cottage cheese; and Sbrinz, a hard Gruyère type. Table cheeses include soft Bel Paese, delicate Fontina, sharp, blue Gorgonzola and, also blue but milder, Dolcelatte. Spicy Provolone is instantly recognisable from its animal or other shapes. Taleggio is mild and creamy, and Mascarpone is a soft, double-cream cheese. Pecorino, the generic name for ewe's milk cheeses, hard and sharp, is used for both cooking and eating.

Formaggi:
CHEESES,
clockwise: Gorgonzola, Parmesan, Mozzarella, Taleggio, Ricotta, Fontina, Dolcelatte, Sbrinz. In the centre, Bel Paese and, top left corner, Provolone

SWEETS, CAKES AND PASTRIES

Traditional desserts are definitely not for the figure-conscious. The Italians gorge themselves on rich pastries, heavy gateaux and rib-sticking concoctions like *Torta Monte Bianco* – chestnut purée with lashings of whipped cream on a meringue base – or the curiously named *Zuppa inglese*, a mixture of sponge cake and liqueur-flavoured trifle with yet more cream. Easier on the digestion are *Pesche farcite*, baked peaches with crushed macaroons, or one of the excellent home-made ice creams (*gelato*). *Cassata alla Siciliana* consists of a sponge cake with ricotta cheese and candied fruit.

1 Cassata
ICE CREAM MOULD
Various coloured ice
cream, with layers of fruit,
nuts and macaroons

2 Zabaglione
HOT EGG AND MARSALA
CUSTARD
One of the most popular
desserts outside Italy, and a
frothy sweet of egg yolks,
sugar and wine beaten over
a slow fire until thickened.
Served with biscuits. In its
homeland, zabaglione is
regarded as a tonic

3 Macedonia di frutta
FRESH FRUIT SALAD
of raspberries and
strawberries, grapes and
bananas, oranges, apples
and pears, steeped in
liqueur-flavoured syrup for
several hours and served
iced. Peaches, apricots,
plums and purple figs can
also be added

3

4

4 Sorbetto di limone
LEMON WATER-ICE
Also known as *granita*,
water-ices were introduced
to the rest of Europe by the
Italians, who still enjoy
refreshing sorbets
flavoured, in addition to
lemon, with coffee, orange,
strawberry or raspberry.

FRUIT

Fresh fruit table decorations may be bowls of juicy plums, figs, cherries and pears, apricots and grapes; or a simple plate of cultivated or tiny wood strawberries

Fresh fruit is commonplace: sun-ripened peaches
and apricots, luscious cherries and sweet grapes.
Musk and cantaloupe melons accompany Parma
ham for a first course and do double duty as a
dessert course, filled perhaps with raspberries in
Marsala. Among the most delicious Italian fruits are
fresh figs, bursting their green or brown skins with
dark crimson flesh and purple, honey-sweet juice.
Tiny wild strawberries from the hills beyond Rome
are eaten, not with cream but with freshly squeezed
orange or lemon juice.

APERITIFS AND WINES

No comparison can justly be made between Italian and French wines, though with the introduction of strict laws, Italian wines labelled D.O.C. can be expected to be of good quality and moderate price. Ordinary table wines range in Italy, as everywhere else, from the rough to the comfortable. They are generally young and do not travel well – for this reason alone it is sensible to experiment with local wines for daily consumption. In the south, try *Lacrima Christi* (literally 'tears of Christ'), from Mount Vesuvius; a light, dry to medium sweet wine, it is better in the white than in the red type.

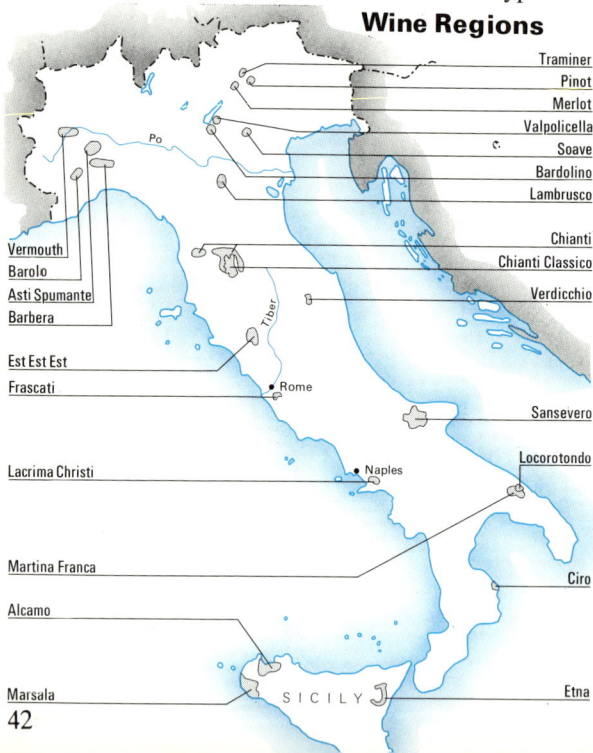

Wine Regions

Traminer
Pinot
Merlot
Valpolicella
Soave
Bardolino
Lambrusco

Chianti
Chianti Classico
Verdicchio

Vermouth
Barolo
Asti Spumante
Barbera

Est Est Est
Frascati

Rome

Sansevero

Locorotondo

Lacrima Christi

Naples

Martina Franca

Ciro

Alcamo

Marsala

SICILY

Etna

1 Aperitivi
   APERITIFS
   are almost synonymous
   with vermouth. *Punt e Mes*
   is dry and bitter-sweet,
   while *Cinzano bianco* and
   Martini rosso are sweet
   vermouths. Bitter *Campari*,
   diluted with soda, is
   steadily increasing in
   popularity

2 Vini bianchi dolci
   WHITE DESSERT WINES:
   Marsala, the fortified sweet
   white wine from Sicily, is
   probably the best known,
   but the golden *Orvieto*
   wines from Umbria are
   equally smooth. Roman
   Frascatis can be robust,
   like the strong *Vin Santo*
   from Tuscany

2

3

3 **Vini bianchi**
WHITE WINES
range from the very dry,
crisp and straw-coloured
*Verdicchio dei Castelli di
Jesi* through the medium
dry *Soave*, delicate or fruity
in superior qualities, and
the medium dry but fruity
Torbato secco from
Sardinia, to the sweet and
sparkling *Asti Spumante*

4

4 **Vini rossi**
RED WINES include the
famous *Chianti* from
Tuscany, light and fruity
when young, full-bodied in
the *Riserva* qualities. From
Piedmont come the strong
and distinctive *Barolo* and
its lighter counterpart
Barbaresco. Veneto
produces *Valpolicella*, a
light and pleasant red, and
Bardolino, lighter and
almost rosé

COFFEE AND LIQUEURS

COFFEE is drunk throughout the day, leisurely at pavement cafes, and as the finale to lunch and dinner. It may be *Caffè espresso* (foreground), frothy *Cappuccino* topped with cocoa or grated chocolate.

It was to Venice, gateway to the East when trading routes were opened up, that the first cargo of coffee beans arrived in the 16th century. Within decades small coffee shops sprang up in the city, and the coffee-drinking habit, if not the Italian expertise, soon spread to the rest of Europe. Today, the Italians are still perfectionists in the art of coffee-making, be it small cups of strong, black *Espresso macchiato* or *Cappuccino*, equally strong but frothy with milk. *Caffè ristretto* is strong coffee, and *Caffè Hag* weak. *Caffè corretto* means coffee with liqueur.

Liquori
LIQUEURS
of Italian parentage include the fiery *Grappa*, made from grape skins and pips; sometimes yellow (Nardini), sometimes white and herby. *Maraschino* is sweeter, from cherries, and *Strega* has a pronounced herb taste. *Amaretto di Saronne* is almond-flavoured, while the clear and sweet *Sambuca* has an aftertaste of anise. *Fernet Branca*, a bitter digestive, includes herbs and orange peel

GLOSSARY OF ITALIAN MENU AND CULINARY TERMS

A

Abbacchio: baby lamb.
al forno: roasted, with rosemary.
alla cacciatora: lamb cubes braised with sage, rosemary, garlic, vinegar and anchovies.
alla Romana: braised in white wine, egg and lemon sauce.

Acciughe: in northern Italy, anchovy. See also Alici.
salsa d': anchovy sauce with chopped green peppers, garlic, parsley and capers; served with poached fish.

Acqua minerale: mineral water.
gassata: sparkling.
naturale: still.

Aglio: garlic.

Agnello: lamb.
all'arrabbiata: braised in tomato and chilli sauce.

Agnolotti al sugo d'arroste: ravioli stuffed with minced meat.

Agrodolce: sweet-sour sauce of vinegar, garlic, bay, bitter chocolate and gravy.

Albicocche: apricot.

Al dente: applied to pasta 'cooked to the bite' and slightly resistant.

Alici: anchovies.

Allodole: larks.

Al sangue: rare (of steak).

Amaretti: small macaroons.

Ananas: pineapple.

Anguilla: eel.
in umido: eel stew with wine, garlic and tomato purée.

Animelle: sweetbreads.
briache: cooked in wine.
d'abbachio al prosciutto: as *briache*, but cooked with ham and Marsala.
di vitello: calf sweetbreads.

Anitra: duck.
arrosto alla Genovese: marinated in oil, roasted and served with pan juices.
in agrodolce: braised in sweet and sour sauce.
in salmi alla Romana: casserole of duck, with giblet sauce and olives.
selvatica: roast wild duck in Marsala sauce.

Anolini di erbette: ravioli stuffed with spinach.

Anzio pie: pasta pie with minced meat, seasoned with orange peel and cinnamon.

Aragosta: crawfish, lobster.

Arancia: oranges.
al caramel: in syrup, garnished with caramelised orange peel.
ripiene: oranges stuffed with strawberries.

Arancini alla Siciliana: Parmesan-flavoured rice balls stuffed with veal, tomatoes and basil; deep-fried.

Aringhe: herrings.

Arista alla Fiorentina: roast loin of pork with garlic and rosemary; served cold.

Arrosto: roast (of meat).

Arselle: clams. See also Vongole.

Asparagi: asparagus; *punti di asparagi*: tips.

B

Baccalà: salted cod.
fresco: haddock.
Bagna cauda: hot sauce or dip
of oil, butter, garlic and
anchovies.
Barbabietote: beetroot.
Barbuta: brill.
Beccaccia: woodcock.
crostini di beccaccia arrosto:
roast woodcock on toast.
Beccaccino: snipe.
Basilico: basil.
Ben cotta: well done (of steak).
Besciamella: béchamel sauce.
Bianchetti: whitebait.
Bianco, in: boiled.
Bicchiere: glass.
Birra: beer.
Bistecca: steak, see also *al
sangue, ben cotta* and *cotta a
puntino*.
alla pizzaiole: with tomato
and garlic sauce.
Fiorentina: porterhouse
steak, charcoal-grilled.
Bollito: Piedmont classic dish
of mixed boiled meats, with
haricot beans and *salsa verde*
con mostarda di Cremona: see
page 29.
Bologna sausage: made from
minced beef and pork, with
sage and garlic.
Bomboline de ricotta in brodo:
soup with ricotta cheese
dumplings.
Bonito: type of small tunny
fish.
Bracioline: cutlets.

Branzino: sea bass.
Brasato: braised meat.
di manzo: braised beef.
alla Bresciana: beef braised
in oil and red wine, with
garlic, bacon and onions.
Bresaola: dried salted beef,
thinly sliced and served with
oil and lemon juice as
antipasto.
Brodetto: fish soup cum stew,
usually with squid, eel, red
mullet, bass and shellfish,
with tomatoes, garlic and
herbs. See also page 21.
Brodo: consommé or broth.
di cappone: chicken
consommé.
di manzo: beef stock.
*pasta in brodo con fegatini e
piselli*: chicken stock with
pasta, peas and chicken
livers.
pasta in brodo e faglioli:
consommé with pasta and
haricot beans.
pasta in brodo e lenticchie:
with pasta and lentils.
Bucatini all'Amatriciana:
spaghetti with bacon, tomato
and chilli sauce.
Budino: pudding, dessert.
di prugne: flan case with
filling of prunes, sultanas,
currants, raisins, sponge
cake, ground nuts, lemon
peel, cream and Marsala.
toscano: baked cheese mould
with almonds, candied peel,
raisins and sultanas.
Burrida: another name for
Brodetto. See also page 21.

Burro: butter.
al burro: cooked in or served with butter.
, salsa di: butter sauce with onion, parsley and wine.

C

Cacciatora, alla: braised in olive oil and white wine, with vegetables and herbs; applied to game and poultry.

Cacciucco Livornese: fish stew with octopus, squid, crabs and small lobsters; cooked in oil and white wine, tomato sauce and garlic.

Calamaretti: baby squid.
del Golfo fritte: deep-fried, from Bay of Biscay.

Calamari: squid.
in umido: see page 20.

Calazione: lunch.

Calzone: Neapolitan speciality of pizza turnovers, with ham and mozzarella cheese filling.

Cannellini: dried haricot beans dressed with oil and vinegar.

Caponata: see page 31.

Capretto: kid.
al forno: roast, with garlic and rosemary.
al vino bianco: braised in white wine and Marsala, with vegetables and herbs.

Capperi: capers.

Capriolo: roe-deer.
alla Valdostana: cooked in white wine and brandy, with cheese and white truffles.

Carciofi: globe artichokes.

alla crèma: in cream sauce.
alla Giudea: young whole artichokes, fried crisp and golden; speciality of Rome.
alla Veneziana: violet-leaved; braised in oil and white wine.
di insalata: sliced, with oil, lemon juice and salt.
ripieni: stuffed with breadcrumbs, anchovies and garlic; braised in wine.

Carne: meat.

Carote: carrots.

Cartoccio: oiled paper or parchment cases in which certain foods are cooked.

Casalinga: home made.

Cassata alla Siciliana: see page 35. Also an ice cream cake (*cassata gelato*).

Castagne: chestnuts.
al Marsala: chestnuts cooked in Marsala and red wine.

Cavolfiori: cauliflower,
saltati al burro e aglio: sautéed in butter and garlic.

Cavolini di Bruxelles: Brussels sprouts.

Cavolo: cabbage.
in agrodolce: in sweet and sour sauce.

Cena: dinner.

Cenci alla Fiorentina: crisp-fried sweet pastries.

Cervello: brains.
al burro nero: in browned butter with vinegar and capers.

Cervo: venison.
con salsa di ciliegii: pot-roasted, with cherry sauce.

Cetrioli: cucumber.

alla dusa: stuffed with eggs, mustard, onions, anchovies and radishes.

Cicoria: chicory.

Cifalo: grey mullet.

Ciliegii: cherries.

Cima di vitello: stuffed breast of lamb.
alla Genovese: stuffed with sweetbreads, artichokes, green peas, Parmesan and herbs; served cold.

Cinghiale: wild boar.
brasato di cinghiale con cipolla: braised boar with onions and wine.

Cioccolato: chocolate.
budino: chocolate mousse.

Cipolla: onions.
ripiene: stuffed with ham, anchovies, garlic, parsley and black olives.

Cipollina: chives.

Cocomero: watermelon.

Cocozelle: type of courgette (zucchini).

Conchiglia: small shellfish.

Coniglio: rabbit.
agrodolce: Sicilian casserole, with sultanas, onions, herbs and pine kernels.
arrosto: roast rabbit.
in padella: Roman casserole, with white wine, bacon, tomatoes and herbs.

Consommé all'uova: beef consommé poured over eggs beaten with lemon juice; served with grated cheese.

Conto: bill.

Coperto: cover charge.

Cosciotti di rane fritte: deep-fried frogs' legs.

Costolette: cutlets.
Bolognese: veal cutlets, topped with ham and Parmesan; also veal escalopes cooked in Marsala.
d'agnello alla Marinetti: lamb cutlets braised in white wine with herbs.
di maiale: pork chops.
vitello alla Milanese: veal cutlets with lemon and parsley.
vitello alla valdostana: see page 29.

Cotechino: rich pork sausage.
con fagioli: boiled and served with haricot beans.

Cotta a puntino: medium-rare (of steak).

Cozze: mussels.
alla marinara: marinated in oil and white wine.
al vino bianco: served cold, in white wine sauce with garlic and parsley.

Crema: cream or custard.
caramella: caramel custard.
di mascarpone: cream cheese (mascarpone), sweetened and flavoured with liqueur; served chilled with cream.
di polla: chicken soup.

Crescione: watercress.

Crespolini: thin pancakes stuffed with spinach, cream cheese, Parmesan and chicken livers; topped with béchamel sauce and cheese.

Crocchette: croquettes.
di cervella: calf's brain.

Crostacei: shellfish.

Crostata: flan.
  di ricotta: cheesecake.
Crostini: bread and cheese
croûtons.
  di provatura (mozzarella):
toasted cheese with
anchovies; popular in
Roman trattoria.
Cupate: honey and nut
pastries.

D, E

Dandelioni: dandelion.
Datteri di mare: sea dates,
small, mussel-like shellfish.
Dattero: date.
Dolce: sweet.
Dolci: desserts, cakes.
  mafarka: coffee, lemon and
orange-flavoured rice mould.
Endivia: endive.
Escaloppe alla Milanese: crisp-
fried veal escalopes with
lemon and parsley. See also
Scaloppe.

F

Fagiano: pheasant.
Fagioli: dried beans.
  all'uccelletto: cooked in olive
oil with tomatoes and garlic.
  toscani col tonne: cooked
dried beans and tunny fish in
salad dressing.
Fagiolini: French beans.
  col tonne: beans and tunny
fish, dressed with oil and
lemon juice.

Farinacei: pasta and rice
dishes.
Fave: broad beans.
  al guanciale: fresh broad
beans cooked in butter with
bacon and onions.
Fegatini: chicken liver.
  , salsa di: sauce of chicken
livers, mushrooms and
Marsala wine.

Fettuccine is the Roman
name for ribbon noodles,
which the Bolognese call
tagliatelle and claim are
cooked and served to
perfection only in the
Emilia region. Whatever
the name, ribbon noodles
belong to the best and
most popular of fresh
home-made egg pastas. In
Bologna, every restaurant
offers *Tagliatelle alla
Bolognese*, with the classic
Ragù so poorly imitated
as Bolognese sauce all
over the world. The
Bolognese themselves
favour *Tagliatelle al
burro*, tossed in plenty of
butter, cream and Parme-
san, which the Romans
offer up as *Fettucine al
doppio burro* or *all'
Alfredo*. The Neapolitan
way with fettucine or tagliatelle is *alla marinara*, in
fresh tomato sauce with
basil.

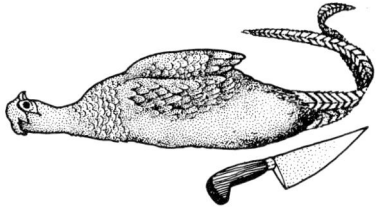

Fegato di vitello: calf's liver.
al burro e salvia: fried with
sage leaves in butter.
alla Veneziana: with onions.
Fichi: figs.
d'India: prickly pears.
Finocchio: fennel.
Fiorentina: garnish or sauce
containing spinach.
Focaccia di pomidoro: savoury
flan with tomatoes, onions,
courgettes, garlic
and sage.
Foiolo: tripe.
Fonduta: cheese fondue, made
with fontina cheese, topped
with sliced white truffles;
speciality of Piedmont.
alla parmigiana: similar, but
with Parmesan cheese.
Formaggio: cheese.
Forno, al: roasted or baked.
Fragoline: strawberries.
di bosco: wild strawberries.
, gelato di: strawberry ice
cream.
di mare: sea strawberries
(tiny baby squid).
Frittata: omelette.
aromatica (al formaggio):
with Parmesan, basil,
marjoram and parsley.
Frittatine imbolitte: savoury
stuffed pancakes.
Fritelle: fritters.
di aragosta: lobster.
di San Giuseppe: sweet rice
fritters with orange and
lemon peel, and Marsala.
Fritto misto: 'mixed fry' of
meat and vegetables, coated
with batter and deep-fried.

alla Fiorentina: sliced chicken
breast, brains, sweetbreads,
artichokes and mozzarella.
di mare: fried seafood (squid,
prawns, red mullet, etc.)
di verdure: sliced aubergines,
courgettes and mozzarella.
Frutta: fruit.
candita: crystallised.
cotta: stewed.
Funghi: mushrooms.
alla graticola: grilled, with
garlic and marjoram.
fritte: deep-fried, in batter.
ripieni: stuffed with bacon,
Parmesan, garlic and herbs.

G

Gamberetti: shrimps, prawns
Gamberi: large prawns.
di fiume: crayfish.
Gambero do mare: true lobster
and rare in Italy; the shellfish
served as lobster is usually
the crawfish, Aragosta.
Gelato: ice cream.
di fragole: strawberry.
al torrone: noûgat.
Genovese, salsa: pasta sauce
from veal, onions, carrots,
tomatoes, dried mushrooms
and white wine.

Ghiaccio: ice.
Giorno, del: (dish) of the day.
Gnocchi: small, cork-shaped
dumplings, usually potato.
alla Piemontese: served in
brown sauce and with
Parmesan cheese.
alla Romana: semolina

dumplings in tomato sauce, grilled with cheese.
con tartufo bianco: with pesto sauce and truffles.
verde: dumplings of spinach and ricotta cheese.
Grana: regional name (Emilia) for Parmesan cheese.
Granchio: crab.
Granita: water-ice or sorbet.
Granoturco: sweet corn.
Gremolata: mixture of finely chopped parsley, garlic and lemon peel, traditionally served with Osso buco.
Griglia, alla: grilled.
Grissini: long breadsticks.

I

Indive: chicory.
al sugo di carne: braised.
Insalata: salad.
condita: dressed salad.
di barbabiètole con granoturco: beetroot and sweet corn.
di frutta di mare: sea-food and mushrooms.
di funghi: raw mushrooms dressed in oil and lemon.
di patate: potatoes, often with capers and anchovies.
di patate col tonne: potatoes, onions and tunny fish.
d'ovuli: egg salad.
verde: green salad.

L

Lampone: raspberries.
Lasagne: large pasta strips, plain or green, flavoured with spinach (*verde*).
al forno (pasticciate): baked lasagne layered with ragù and béchamel sauce.
alla Piemontese: similar, with sliced white truffles.
Latte: milk.
Lattuga: lettuce.
Lenticchie: lentils.
in umido: cooked in oil, with onions, garlic and mint.
Lepre: hare.
alla montana: casserole with red wine, sugar, cinnamon, pine kernels and sultanas.
Limone: lemon.
Lingua: tongue.
di bue: ox tongue.
con salsa verde: cold ox tongue with dressing of oil and lemon juice, capers, anchovies and parsley.
Lonza: Cured fillet of pork flavoured with spices, garlic and wine; served raw as antipasto.
Lumache: snails.
in zimino: cooked in oil, with mushrooms, garlic, onions, parsley and rosemary.

M

Maccheroni: macaroni.
al forno: baked, with

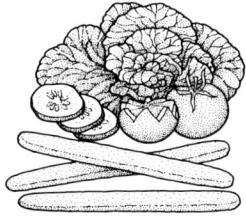

tomatoes, mushrooms and
cheese, with béchamel sauce.
alla carbonara: mixed with
diced ham, lightly scrambled
eggs and Parmesan cheese;
speciality of Rome.
alla chitarra: thin pasta
strips, cut with fine wire
strings – hence the name
meaning guitar strings –
speciality of Ambruzzi
region; served dressed with
oil and diced pepper.
alla Napolitana: with a sauce
of tomatoes, bacon, onions,
garlic, carrots and basil.
alla Siciliana: baked, with
layers of aubergines and
ricotta cheese, topped with
egg and cheese mixture.
Macedonia di frutta: fruit
salad.
Maiale: pork.
al latte: herb-flavoured loin
of pork cooked in milk.
costa di maiale alla griglia:
chops marinated in oil,
fennel, garlic, juniper berries,
then grilled.
ubriaco: pork chops in red
wine.
Maionese: mayonnaise.
tonnata: with tunny fish.
verde: mixed with parsley or
basil, pine kernels and
pistachio nuts.
Mandarino: tangerine.
Mandorle: almonds.
Manzo: beef.
al vino rosso, costa di: rib of
beef marinated and cooked in
red wine.

bollito: boiled beef.
Marasca: morello cherry.
Maritozzi: raisin, candied peel
and pine kernel yeast buns.
Mazzancolle: large prawns,
similar to scampi.
Melanzane: aubergines.
alla parmigiana: baked with
Parmesan and mozzarella
cheese.
ripiene: stuffed with
anchovies, black olives,
garlic, capers and herbs.
Mele: apples.
Messicani di vitello: see page
27.
Migliaccio: bread made from
chestnut flour thickly
sprinkled with pine kernels;
served with small grilled
game birds.
Minestra: collective term for
thick vegetable soups.
fredde: chilled.
al pomidoro: tomato soup.
di funghi: mushroom soup.
Torinese: mixed vegetable
soup, flavoured with garlic
and saffron.
Minestrone: Italy's national
soup, with numerous regional
variations. Typically it
contains dried beans, turnips,
cabbage, peas, carrots,
tomatoes, bacon or gammon,
pasta or rice. Garnished with
small pasta and served with
grated Parmesan.
alla Milanese: made with
salted pork, dried and fresh
beans, cabbage and rice.
Genovese: with Pesto.

Monte Bianco: mound of sweetened chestnut purée with whipped cream.

Mortadella: large pork sausage flavoured with coriander; speciality of Bologna.

Mozzarella in carrozza: mozzarella cheese sandwiches dipped in egg and fried in oil. *Milanese:* fingers of mozzarella cheese, coated with egg and breadcrumbs; fried in oil.

N, O

Napolitana: with tomatoes and basil.

Noce: walnut.
di cocco: coconut.
, salsa di: walnut, oil, parsley and cream sauce.

Oca: goose.

Olio di oliva: olive oil.

Oliva: olive.

Olivette glacate: veal roll stuffed with ham, Parmesan and parsley.

Ortaggi: vegetable dishes.

Osso buco: shin of veal, chopped into pieces and cooked in wine and stock with tomatoes; garnished with Gremolata and served with Risotto alla Milanese.

Ostriche: oysters.
alla Veneziana: oysters with caviar.

P

Paesana, salsa: pasta sauce of mushrooms, bacon and Parmesan cheese.

Pallottole d'aranci: dessert of orange and lemon peel fondant balls covered with chopped nuts.

Palombacci: wood pigeons. *alla perugina:* spit-cooked, served with giblet sauce with red wine and olives.

Pan di spagna: sponge cake.

Pane: bread.
tostato: toast.

Panettone: yeast cake with raisins and candied peel; traditional at major religious festivals.

Panforte: spicy honey cake with almonds, walnuts, candied peel and chocolate; speciality of Siena.

Panna: cream
montata: whipped cream.

Panzanella alla marinara: salad of crumbled bread and herbs, with dressing of hard-boiled egg yolks, garlic and anchovies.

Pappa col pomodoro: bread and tomato soup.

Pappardelle: broad, crimped noodles.
all'arrabbiata: with sauce of bacon, tomatoes and chillis.
con la lepre: with hare, wine and cheese sauce.

Parmigiana: Parmesan cheese.

Passatelli: chicken or beef

consommé with small cheese balls.

Passato: purée.
di legume: thin, strained vegetable soup.
di patate: creamed potatoes.

Pasta: paste made from flour, water and, often, eggs. The staple food, particularly in southern Italy; in the north, rice and polenta dishes replace the pasta (see also pages 14–17).
asciutta: literally dry pasta, a collective term for pasta.
con le sarde: pasta with sauce of tomatoes, salted sardines, onions, pine kernels, sultanas, saffron and fennel; speciality of Sicily.
e lenticchie: see Brodo.
frolla: sweet shortcrust pastry.

Patate: potatoes.
al latte: cooked in milk.

Pebronata: braised beef with juniper berries; Corsican speciality.

Penne: short pasta tubes.
all'arrabbiata: with sauce of bacon, tomatoes and chillis.

Peperata, salsa: sauce of beef marrow and Parmesan.

Peperonata: vegetable dish of red peppers and tomatoes in oil; served hot or cold.

Peperoncini: small chilli peppers.
in padella: braised in white wine with bacon, tomatoes and parsley.

Peperoni: sweet peppers.

con alici e capperi: salad of peppers with anchovies and capers.
ripieni: see page 31.
conserva di peperoni: preserved with basil.

Pere: pears.
al forno caramellata: baked pears in syrup.
ripiene: baked; stuffed with ground almonds and crystallised fruit.

Pernice: partridge.
alla zabaglione: roast, served with fluffy egg and Marsala sauce.

Pesce: fish.

Pesche: peaches.
farcite (ripiene): baked, stuffed with macaroons.

Pesto: cold sauce of garlic, basil, Parmesan and pecorino cheese, pine kernels and oil; served with pasta. Speciality of Genoa.

Petti di pollo: chicken breast.
alla Bolognese: fried, with ham and Parmesan.
alla Cavour: similar, with added white truffles.

Piatti da farsi: dishes cooked to order.

Piatto del giorno: dish of the day.

Piccante, salsa: piquant sauce of red wine, oil, vinegar, garlic and herbs.

Piccate: small thin squares of veal (see Scaloppine), fried in butter and dressed with lemon juice.
al Marsala: similar, but

served with pan juices and Marsala.

Piccioni: pigeons.
col piselli: braised in white wine with tongue, ham and green peas.

Pinoli (pignoli): pine kernels. Also *pinocchio*.

Pimentos: large, sweet red and green peppers.

Piselli: green peas.
al burro: cooked in butter.
al prosciutto (alla Romana): cooked in butter with onions and diced ham.

Pitte con niepita: small sweet pastries filled with grape jam, almonds and grated chocolate.

Pizzaiola: sauce of chopped tomatoes, cooked in oil with garlic and herbs.

Polenta: porridge made from maize flour; staple food in northern Italy.

Polipetto: octopus.

Pollastrino: spring chicken.

Pollo: chicken.
all'aretina: cooked in white wine with peas and rice.
alla Bolognese arrosto: roasted, with ham, tomatoes, garlic and rosemary.
alla cacciatora: see page 25.
alla créma: cooked in cream with brandy.
alla diavolo: charcoal-grilled.
alla Napolitana: casserole with mushrooms, onions, garlic and tomato purée.
in umido: stew with green peppers, onions, tomatoes, mushrooms and green olives.
ripieno arrosto: roast, stuffed with chicken liver and Parmesan cheese.
tonnato: cold boiled chicken dressed with tunny fish mayonnaise.

Pizza: national dish, with numerous regional variations; basically a savoury yeast dough flan with different toppings.
alla francescane: with mushrooms, ham, tomatoes and cheese.
alla Liguria: with anchovies or sardines, onions, tomatoes and black olives.
alla Romana: with onions.
margherita: see page 19.
Napoletana: see page 19.
rustica: shortcrust pizza with ham, Parmesan and cream cheese, and chopped eggs in béchamel sauce.
Siciliana: with tomato purée, onions and anchovy fillets or smoked sausage.
quattro stagioni: topping in 4 sections (for the four seasons): 1) seafood; 2) tomatoes and anchovies; 3) mozzarella and Parmesan with tomatoes and oregano; 4) tomatoes, anchovies and capers.

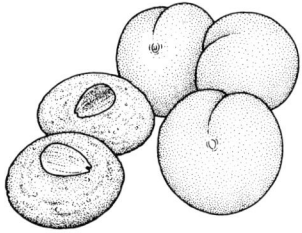

Polpetti: type of thin beef burgers, with garlic, lemon peel and parsley.
di baccala: salted codburgers.
Polpettini: small savoury dumplings.
alla Fiorentina: meat rissoles with artichokes.
di formaggio: deep-fried cheese balls.
di spinaci: spinach and cheese dumplings.
Polpo: octopus.
Pomidori: tomatoes.
ammollicati: baked with topping of breadcrumbs, parsley and garlic.
col tonno: stuffed with tunny fish mayonnaise.
ripieni alla casalinga: baked with meat and vegetable stuffing.
, salsa di: tomato sauce, flavoured with basil.
Pompelmo: grapefruit.
Porchetta: roast sucking pig.
Porri: leeks.
lessati al burro fuso: cooked in butter.
Pranzo: lunch.
Prezzemolo: parsley.
Prezzo fisso: fixed-price menu.
Prima colazione: breakfast.
Prosciutto: ham.
cotto: boiled.
crudo: raw, especially cured Parma ham.
di Parma e melone: Parma ham with melon; *e fichi*: with fresh figs.
Punta di vitello arrosto: roast shoulder of veal.

Q

Quaglia: quail.
alla Milanese: sautéed, coated in breadcrumbs and grated Parmesan cheese.
alla Rossini: boned and roasted; served on goose liver slices, garnished with truffles and with Madeira sauce.
arrosto con polenta: roast, served on fried polenta.
con risotto: see page 25.

R

Rafano: horseradish.
Radici: radishes; also *ravanelli*.
Raddicchio rossa (di Treviso): red-leaved chicory or celery.
Ragù: pasta sauce also called Salsa Bolognese. Made from minced beef, chicken livers, ham, carrots, onion, celery, tomato purée, white wine and seasoning.
Rane: frogs.
in guazzetto: frogs' legs in white wine.
zuppa di rana: frogs' legs and tomato soup.
Rape: turnip.
Ravioli: collective term for stuffed pasta squares.
alla Caprese: stuffed with cheese and herbs; fried.
alla Genovese: stuffed with spinach, veal, Parmesan and herbs.
di ricotta: with ricotta and

Parmesan cheese.
di spinachi: stuffed with spinach and Parmesan.
Razza: skate.
Ribes nero: black currants.
Ribes rosso: red currants.
Ricci: sea-urchins.
Ricotta al caffé: sweetened ricotta cheese flavoured with coffee and rum.
Rigatoni: short ribbed macaroni.
Risi e bisi: Venetian dish of rice and green peas, served with Parmesan.
Riso: rice.
in bianco: plain boiled.
verdi: baked layers of rice, spinach and green pea purée, topped with ground pistachio nuts.
Risotto: basically buttered rice cooked with onions in white wine and water (*bianco*).
alla certosina: with peas, tomatoes, Parmesan and shrimps, flamed with brandy.
alla Genovese: with onions, carrots, celery, beef and veal.
alla Milanese (risotto bianco): with beef marrow cooked in white wine, saffron, butter and cheese, traditional with Osso Buco.
con tartufi d'Alba: with Parmesan and butter, topped with sliced raw truffles.
di peoci: with mussels.
nero: with cuttlefish, and black.
primavera: with chicken livers and spring vegetables.

Rognoni: kidneys.
trifolati: braised veal kidneys in wine or Marsala.
Rolé: rolled stuffed meat.
di manzo: beef stuffed with prosciutto and sage; braised in white wine.
di vitello: veal stuffed with eggs, mortadella, cheese and parsley; cooked in milk.

S

Salame (salami): spiced and smoked sausage; numerous regional varieties.
Salmone: salmon.
Salsa: sauce.
per insalata: salad dressing of oil and lemon juice. See also agrodolce, bagna cauda, besciamella, burro, fegatini, Genovese, maionese, noce, paesana, peperata, pesto, pizzaiola, pomidori, ragù, sugo, tonno and verde.
Sarde, sardelle: sardines.
Salsiccie: fresh sausage, usually pork; spicy.
Saltato: sautéed.
Saltimbocca alla Romana: veal, ham and sage rolls cooked in Marsala.
Salvia: sage.
Scaloppe: escalopes of veal.
farcite: with ham and Gruyère cheese.
Milanese: coated with egg and breadcrumbs; fried.
Scaloppine: small thin escalopes of veal.

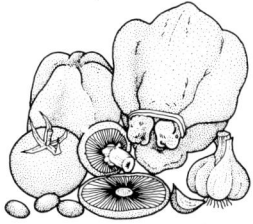

al Marsala: quick-fried in butter and wine.

al limone: in lemon juice.

Scarola: curly endive.

ripiene: stuffed with olives, anchovies, pine kernels, capers, sultanas and garlic; braised in oil and wine.

Scrippelle imbusse: pancakes with ham and cheese.

Secco: dry.

Sedano: celery

gratinati al parmigiano: braised, grilled with Parmesan cheese.

rapo: celeriac.

Senape: mustard.

Servizio compreso: service included.

Sfogliatelle: pastry shells with sweet ricotta cheese.

Sgombo: mackerel.

Sogliola: sole.

alla Veneziana: grilled fillets stuffed with mint, parsley and garlic butter.

al vino bianco: baked in white wine.

Sorbetto: soft ice cream.

di limone: lemon.

Spada: swordfish.

alla graticola: marinated in oil and lemon juice and grilled.

Spiedo, alla: spit-cooked.

Spigola: sea bass.

Spaghetti: common, thin pasta.

al burro: mixed with butter and grated cheese.

all'aglio e olio: with garlic and olive oil.

alla Bolognese: with Ragù

and grated Parmesan.

alla carbonara: with bacon and eggs.

alla marinara (con le acciughe): with tomato, garlic, onion, oil, anchovy and herb sauce.

all'olio e all'uovo: mixed with oil and raw egg.

alla vongole: with clams and tomato sauce.

con salsa di zucchini: with courgettes.

e finocchi alla Siciliana (con le sarde): with fennel, onions, sardines, raisins and pine kernels.

Spinaci: spinach.

all'acciughe: cooked with garlic and anchovies.

al olio e limone: tossed in oil and lemon juice.

Spumanti: sparkling (wine).

Stecche, alla: skewered.

Stracciatella: rich meat broth with beaten eggs and Parmesan mixture which separates to fine strands.

Struffoli: honey-flavoured pastry puffs.

Stufato: marinated beef, casseroled with vegetables in red wine.

di vitello: with veal.

Sugo: juice.

di carne: meat sauce.

di limone: lemon juice.

Suppli: deep-fried rice croquettes.

al telefono: similar, with bel paese or mozzarella cheese in rice mixture.

T

Tacchino: turkey.
arrosta ripieno: roast, stuffed with veal, chestnuts, prunes, turkey liver and Parmesan.
stufato al vino bianco: braised in white wine.

Tagliatelle: flat strips of egg pasta (ribbon noodles).
al ragù: with ragù sauce.
al pesto: with pesto sauce.

Tartufi: truffles.
bianco: white truffles.
di mare: sea truffles, raw.
neri: black.

Tonno: tunny (tuna) fish.
, salsa di: hot sauce, with parsley, butter and stock; served with rice and pasta.

Tordi: thrushes.

Torrone: noûgat.
molle: soft noûgat.

Torta: flan or tart.
di mele alla casalinga: home-made apple flan.
di ricotta: flan with filling of sweetened ricotta cheese, currants and candied peel.
di riso: rice pudding with almonds and crystallised fruit; served cold.

Tortellini: stuffed pasta coils.
di spinaci e ricotta: with spinach and ricotta, flavoured with sage; tossed in melted butter.

Tortini: savoury croquettes.

Triglia: red mullet.

Trippa: tripe.
alla Fiorentina: in tomato sauce and Parmesan.
alla parmigiana: fried, served with melted Parmesan.
alla Romana: braised with tomatoes, carrots, garlic white wine and herbs.
, minestre di: pickled tripe soup.

Trota: trout.

U

Uccelletti: collective term for small edible birds.
di campagna: small beef rolls, skewered and grilled.

Uova: egg.
affogate: poached.
al burro: buttered.
al piatto con pomidoro: baked en cocotte on tomato purée.
alla casalinga: baked in tomatoes.
bazzotte: soft-boiled.
di pesce: hard fish roe.
Fiorentina: baked, with spinach, anchovies and cheese.
ripiene: stuffed.
sode: hard-boiled.
stracciate (strapazzati): scrambled.

Uva: grape.
di corinto: currant.
passa: raisin.
sultane: sultana.
sultane passolina: brandy soaked sultanas wrapped in lemon leaves.

V

Ventagli: fan-shaped puff pastries.

Verde, salsa: green sauce or dressing of olive oil and lemon juice, with garlic, capers and plenty of parsley, sometimes anchovies.
al rafano: with added tomatoes and grated horseradish.

Verdura: vegetable dishes.

Vermicelli: fine spaghetti, usually a soup garnish. Also served with clam and tomato sauce (*alli vongole*).

Verze: cabbage.
ripiene: stuffed cabbage leaves.

Vitello: veal.
alla Genovese: with artichokes in white wine.
tonnato: boned braised leg of veal, served cold with tunny fish mayonnaise.

Vongole: clams.
alla marinara: with garlic and parsley.

Z

Zabaglione (zabaione): frothy dessert of beaten egg yolks, sugar and Marsala. Served warm in glasses or as a hot dessert sauce; also frozen to ice-cream (*zabaglione gelato*). See also page 36.

Zafferano: saffron.

Zamponi: smoked pig's trotters stuffed with minced pork and truffles.
con lentricchie: with stewed lentils.

Zanzarelle: meat broth with fine egg-and-flour strands and Parmesan. See also Stracciatella.

Zimino: fish stew cooked in olive oil, with onions, celery, spinach and herbs.

Zite: large tube pasta.

Zucchine: courgettes.
alla Milanese: sliced, dipped in egg and breadcrumbs and sautéed.
alla Napoletana: baked with tomatoes and mozzarella.
fritte: sliced, coated with batter and fried.

Zuppa: soup.
alla Genovese: fish soup.
alla Pavese: rich beef broth poured over toasted bread with poached eggs and grated cheese.
di castagne: chestnut and celery soup.
di ceci: eel soup.
di cozze: mussels soup·
di fave: garlic-flavoured dried broad bean soup.
di peoci: Venetian mussel soup with garlic.
di pomidoro: tomato soup.
di verdure: mixed vegetable soup with cheese.

Zuppa inglese: Dessert trifle-cake, elaborately decorated with whipped cream and crystallised fruit.

ACKNOWLEDGEMENTS

Photography
All photographs were supplied by the
Anthony Blake Photo Library

Artists
Stonecastle Graphics
Line map by Cox Cartographic

The publishers also wish to acknowledge the help given by
G. Belloni & Co.
Enotria Wines
Gino's Restaurant
San Frediano's Restaurant
Spice of Life

Typesetting by MS Filmsetting Limited, Frome, Somerset
Printed in Great Britain by Balding & Mansell, Wisbech, Cambridge